HAL•LEONARD®

GUITAR PLAY-ALONG

AUDIO
ACCESS
INCLUDED

PLAYBACK+
Speed • Pitch • Balance • Loop

GEORGE HARRISON

Photograph by Terry O'Neill © Umlaut Corporation

To access audio visit:
www.halleonard.com/mylibrary

Enter Code
8101-0501-7521-9844

ISBN 978-1-4950-9786-7

HAL•LEONARD®

Visit Hal Leonard Online at
www.halleonard.com

Contact Us:
Hal Leonard
7777 West Bluemound Road
Milwaukee, WI 53213
Email: info@halleonard.com

In Europe contact:
Hal Leonard Europe Limited
Distribution Centre, Newmarket Road
Bury St Edmunds, Suffolk, IP33 3YB
Email: info@halleonardeurope.com

In Australia contact:
Hal Leonard Australia Pty. Ltd.
4 Lentara Court
Cheltenham, Victoria, 3192 Australia
Email: info@halleonard.com.au

Blow Away

Words and Music by George Harrison

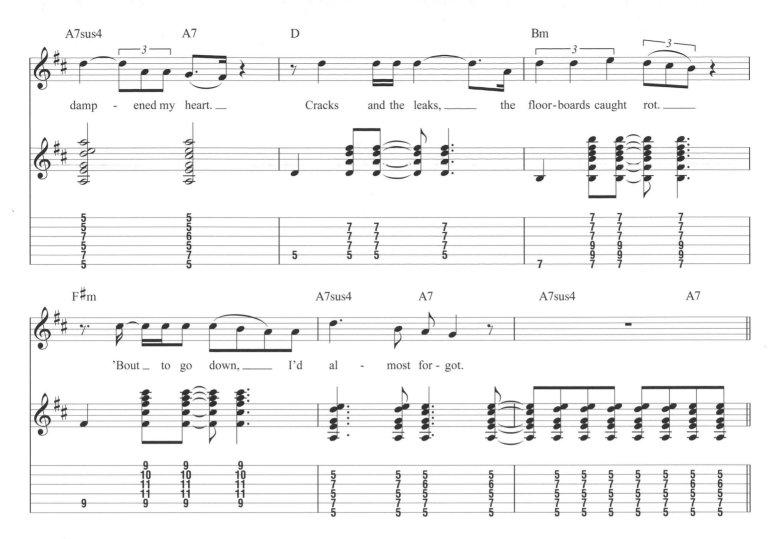

Guitar Solo

Chorus

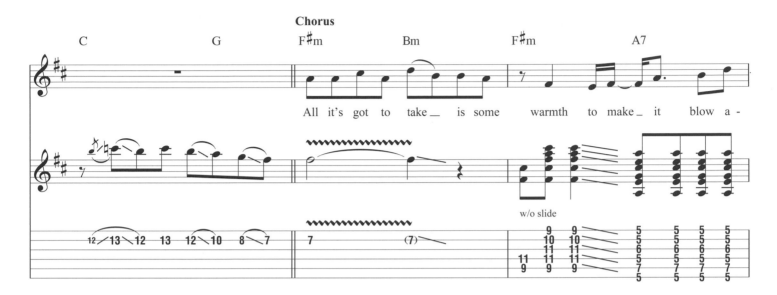

All it's got to take _ is some warmth to make _ it blow a-

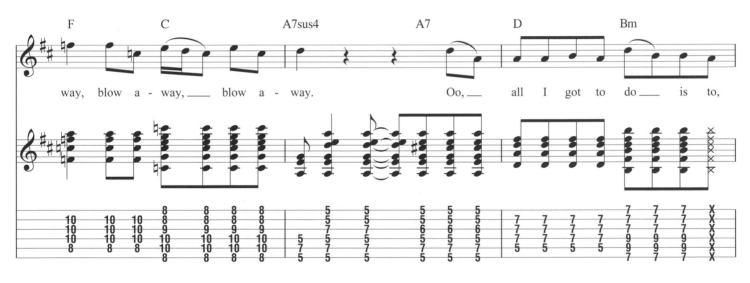

way, blow a-way, ___ blow a-way. Oo, ___ all I got to do ___ is to,

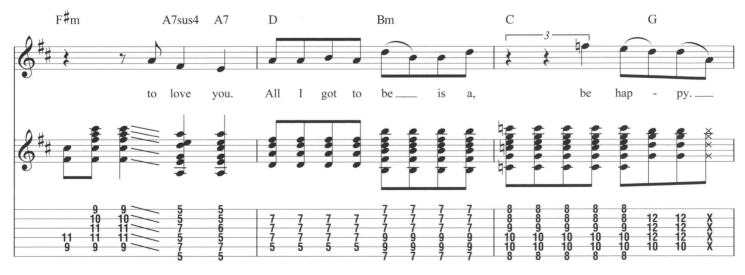

to love you. All I got to be ___ is a, be hap - py. ___

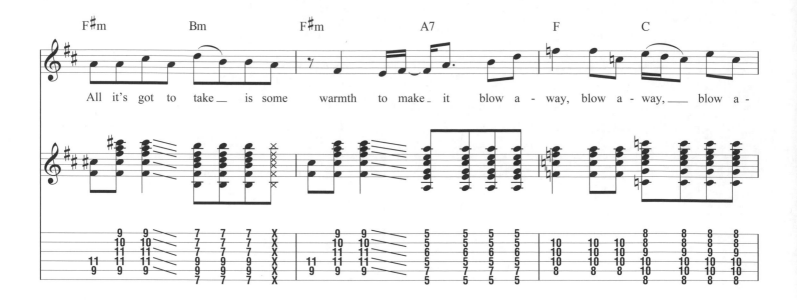

All it's got to take is some warmth to make it blow a-way, blow a-way, blow a-

Outro

way.

Begin fade

Fade out

Additional Lyrics

2. Sky cleared up, day turned to bright.
   Closing both eyes, the head filled with light.
   Hard to remember the state I was in.
   Instant amnesia; Yang to the Yin.

3. Wind blew in, cloud was dispersed.
   Rainbows appearing, the pressures were burst.
   Breezes are singing, now feeling good.
   Moment had passed like I knew that it should.

My Sweet Lord

Words and Music by George Harrison

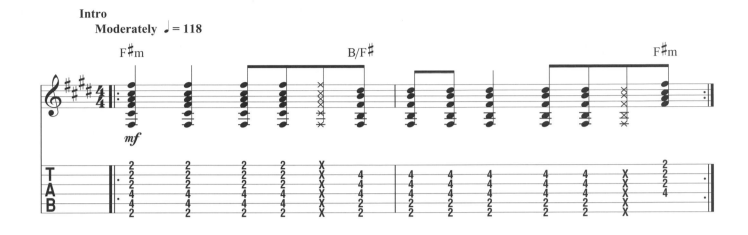

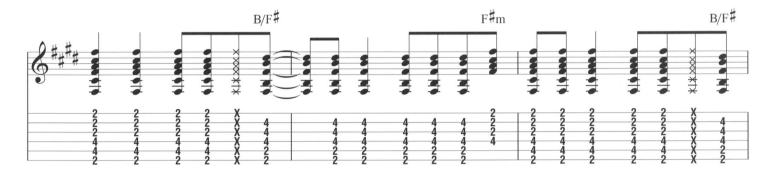

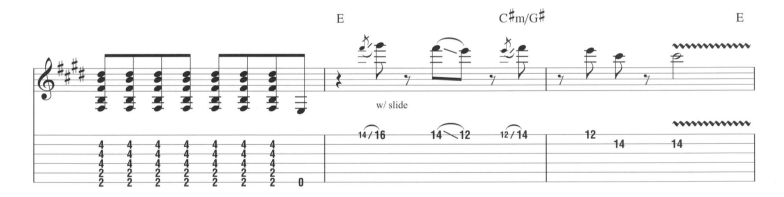

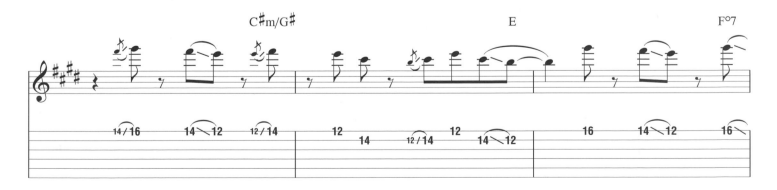

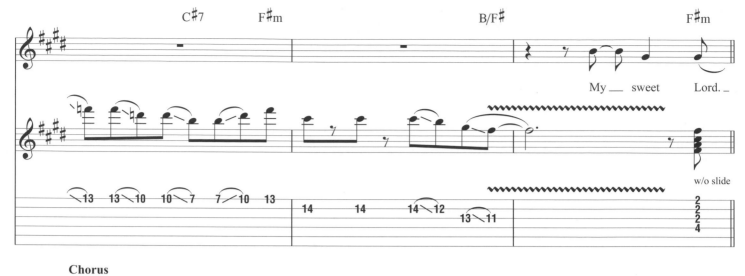

Chorus

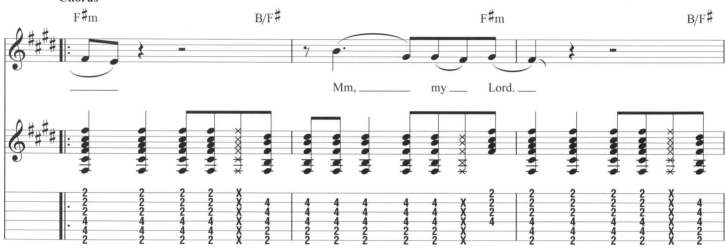

Verse

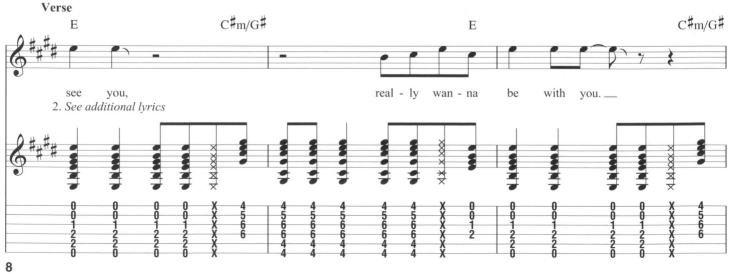

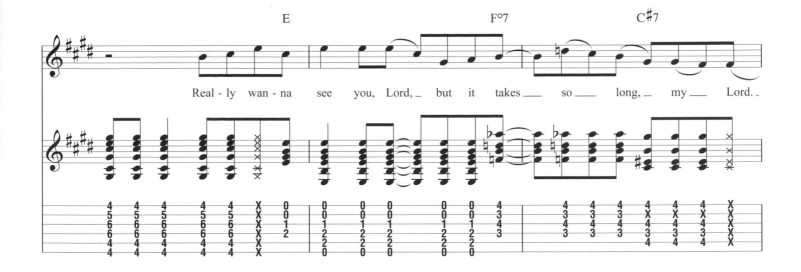

Real - ly wan - na see you, Lord,_ but it takes _ so _ long, my _ Lord._

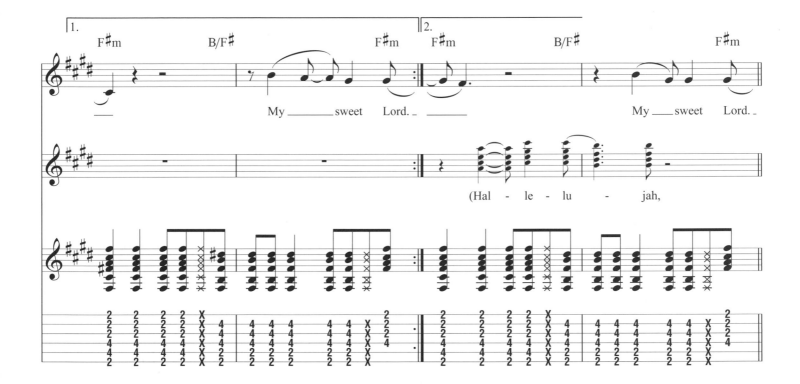

My _ sweet Lord. _

(Hal - le - lu - jah,

My _ sweet Lord. _

Chorus

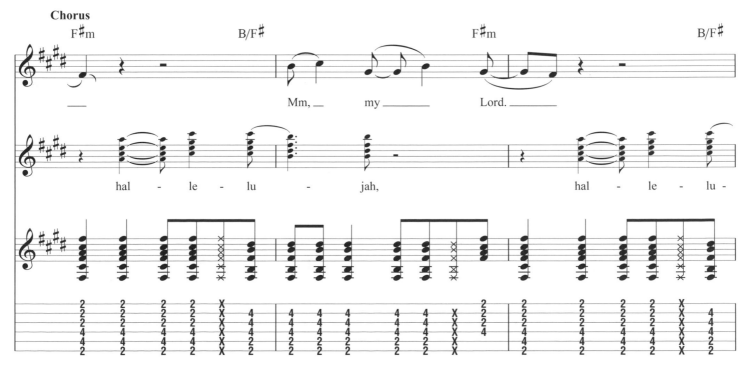

Mm, _ my _ Lord. _

hal - le - lu - jah,

hal - le - lu -

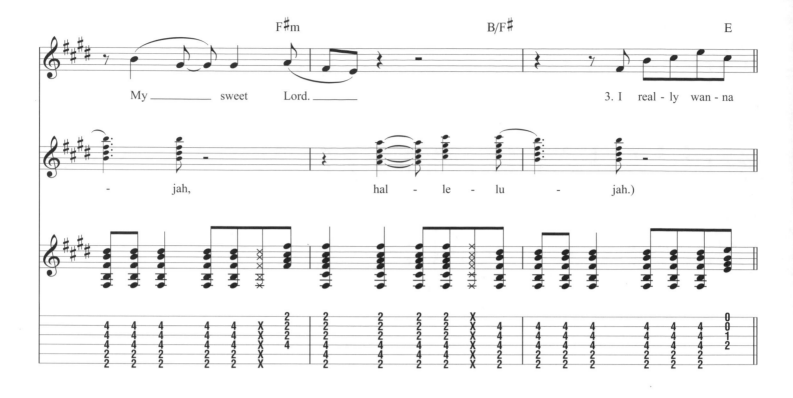

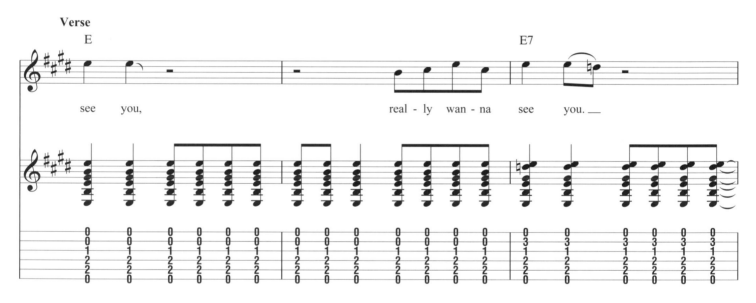

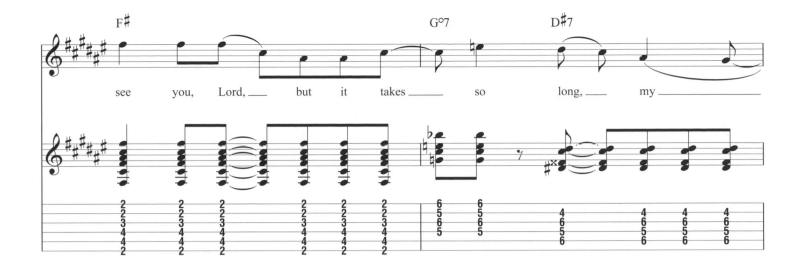

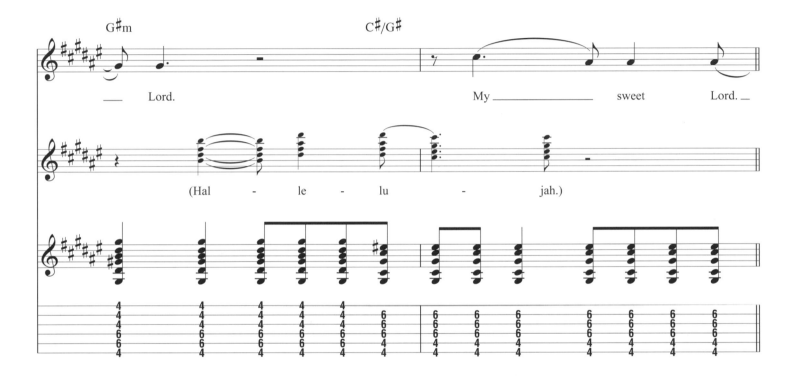

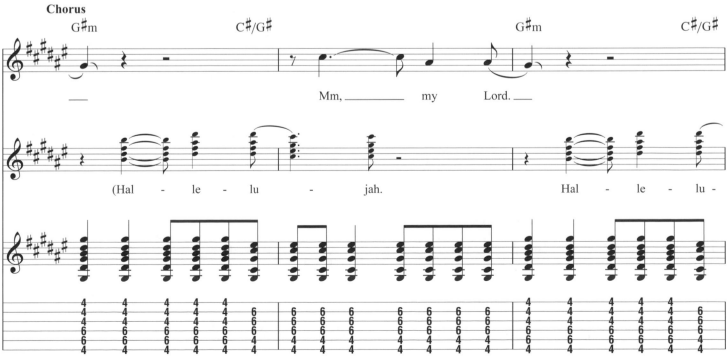

Guitar Solo

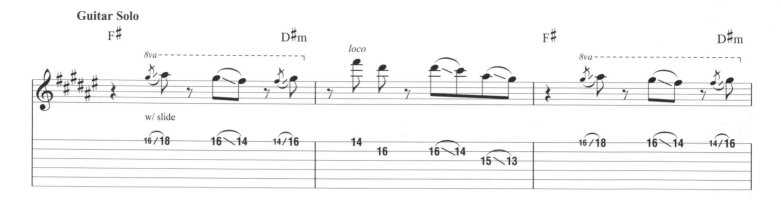

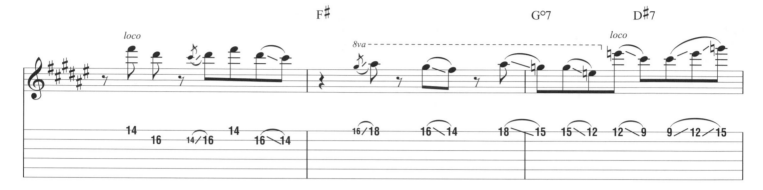

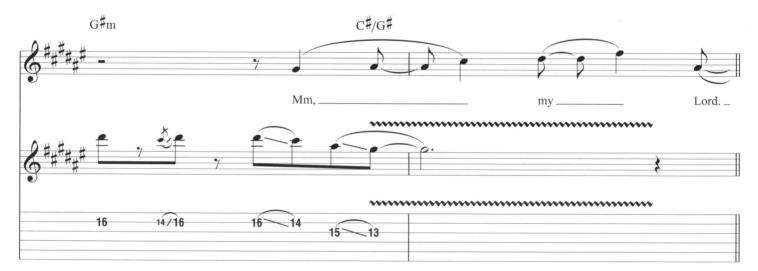

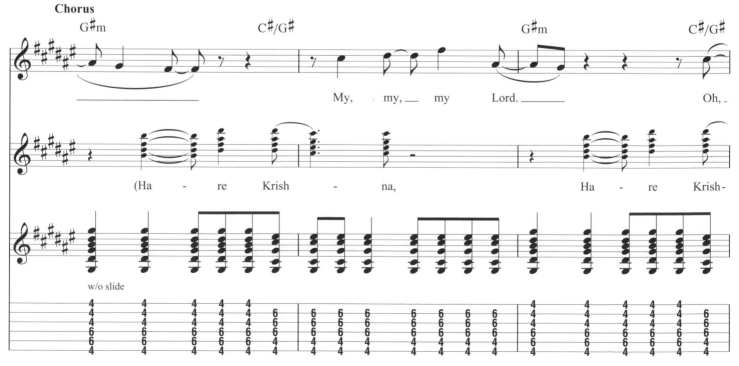

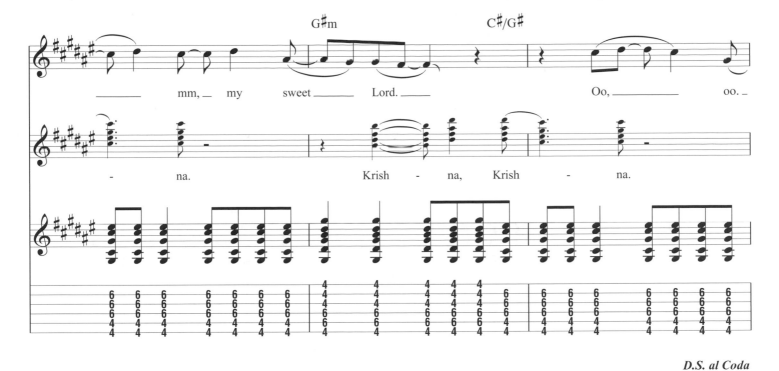

D.S. al Coda

Coda

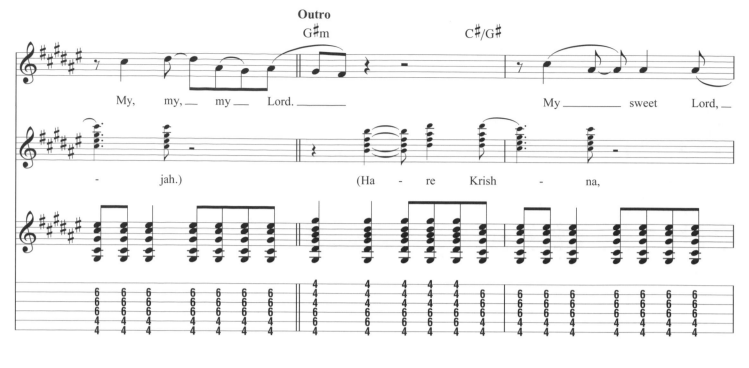

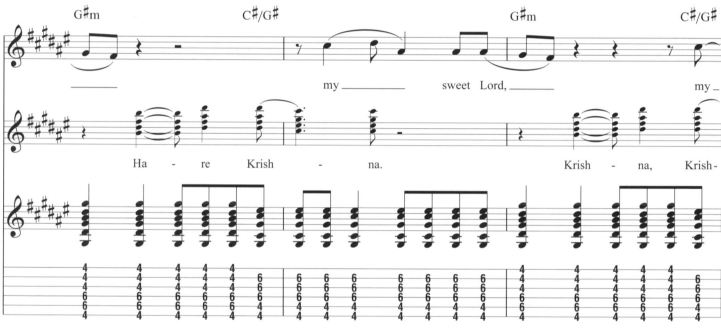

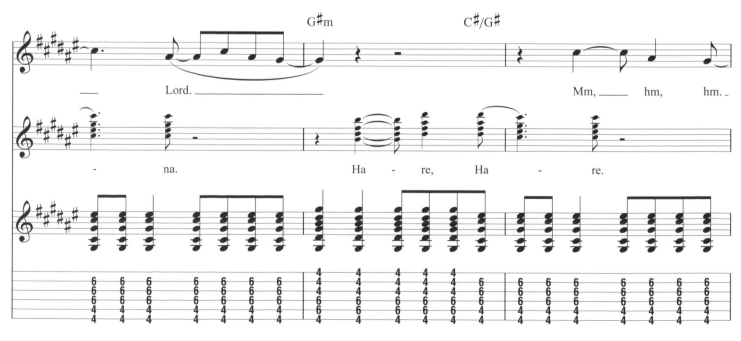

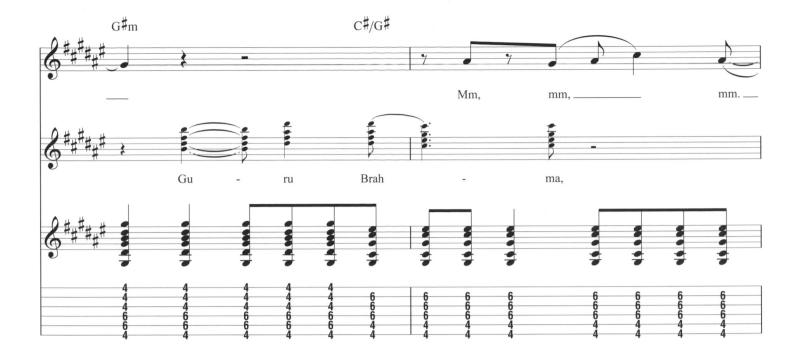

Mm, mm, _____ mm. _____

Gu - ru Brah - ma,

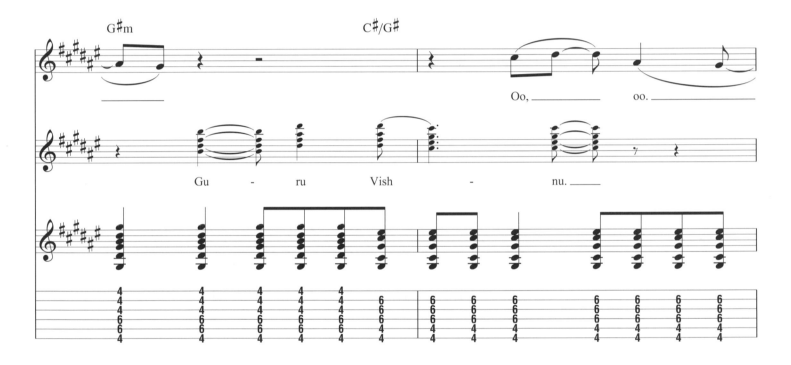

Oo, _____ oo. _____

Gu - ru Vish - nu. _____

w/ Voc. ad lib., till fade

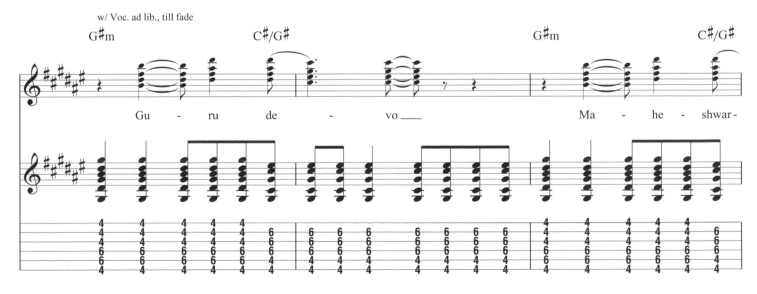

Gu - ru de - vo _____ Ma - he - shwar-

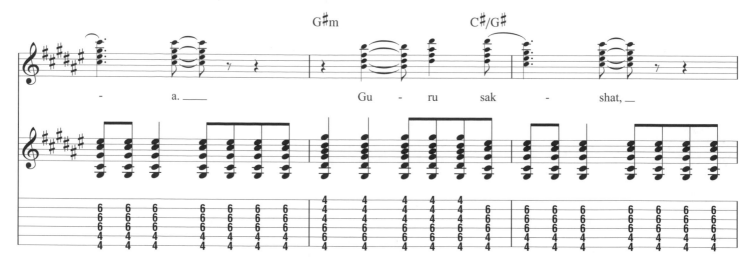

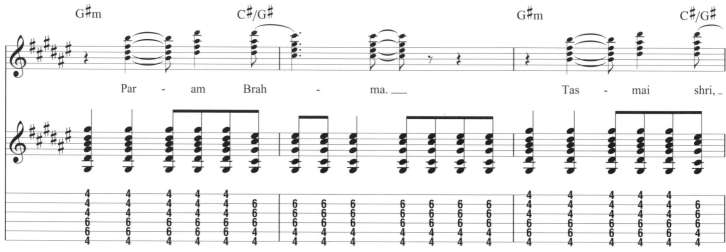

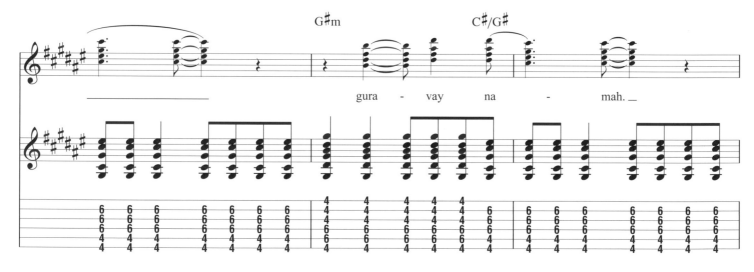

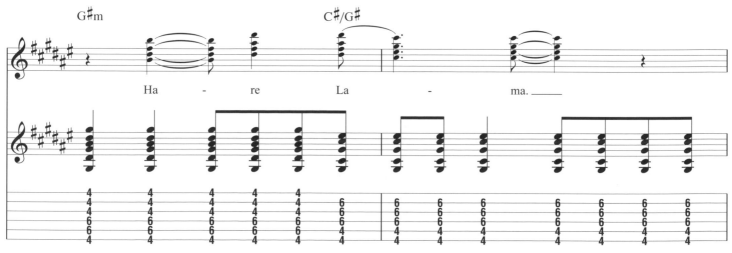

Begin fade

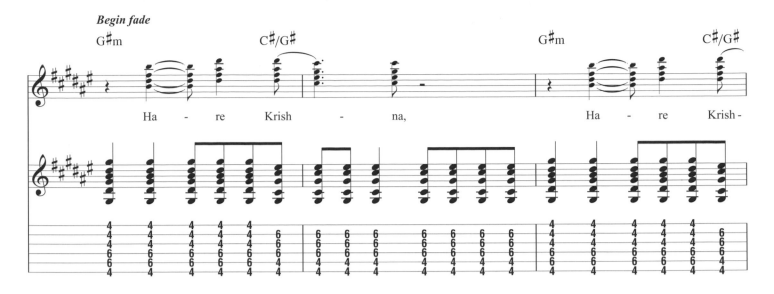

Ha - re Krish - na, Ha - re Krish -

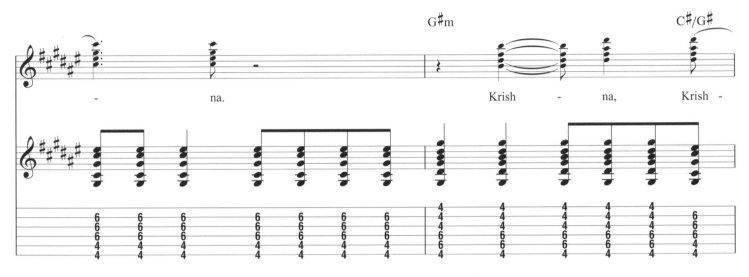

- na. Krish - na, Krish -

Fade out

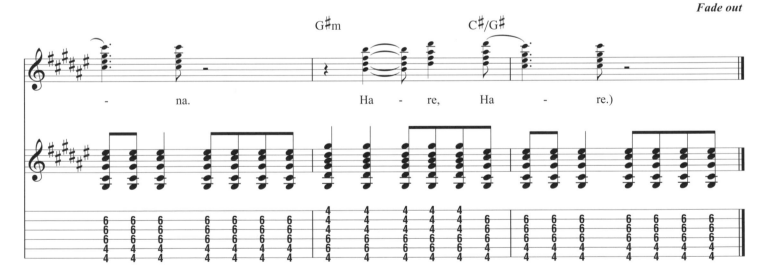

- na. Ha - re, Ha - re.)

Additional Lyrics

2. I really wanna know you,
   Really wanna go with you.
   Really wanna show you, Lord,
   That it won't take long, my Lord.

5. Now, I really wanna see you, (Hare Lama.)
   Really wanna be with you. (Hare Lama.)
   Really wanna see you, Lord, (Ah.)
   But it takes so long, my Lord. (Hallelujah.)
   Mm, my Lord. (Hallelujah.)

Give Me Love
(Give Me Peace on Earth)

Words and Music by George Harrison

Capo III

Intro
Moderately slow ♩ = 79

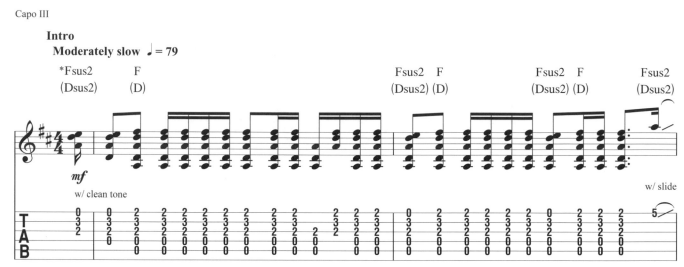

*Symbols in parentheses represent chord names respective to capoed guitar.
Symbols above reflect actual sounding chords. Capoed fret is "0" in tab.

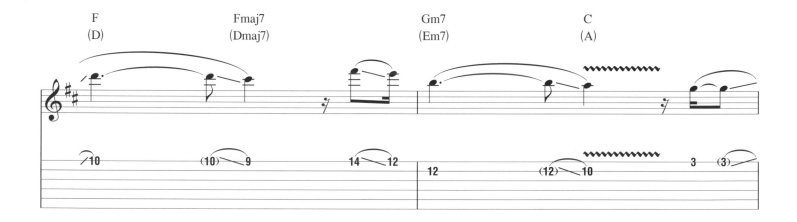

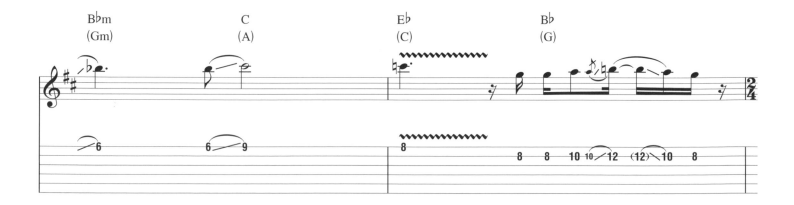

Chorus

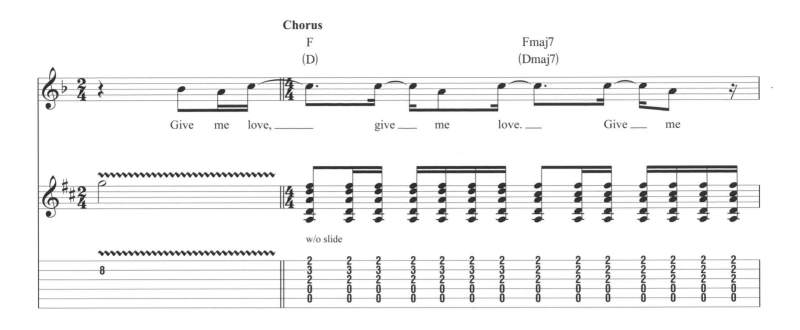

Give me love, _____ give __ me love. __ Give __ me

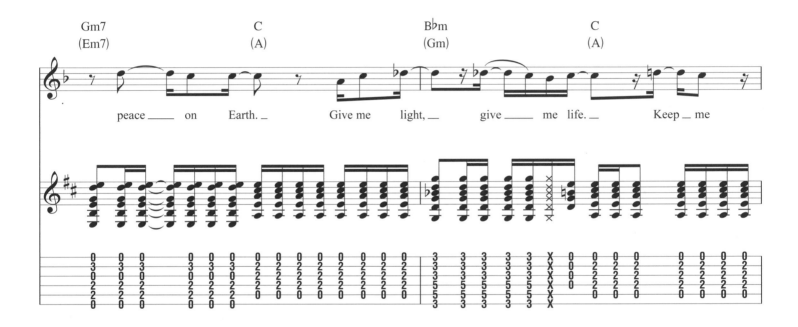

peace ____ on Earth. _ Give me light, _ give ___ me life. _ Keep _ me

free ____ from birth. _ Give _ me hope, help me cope _ with _ this

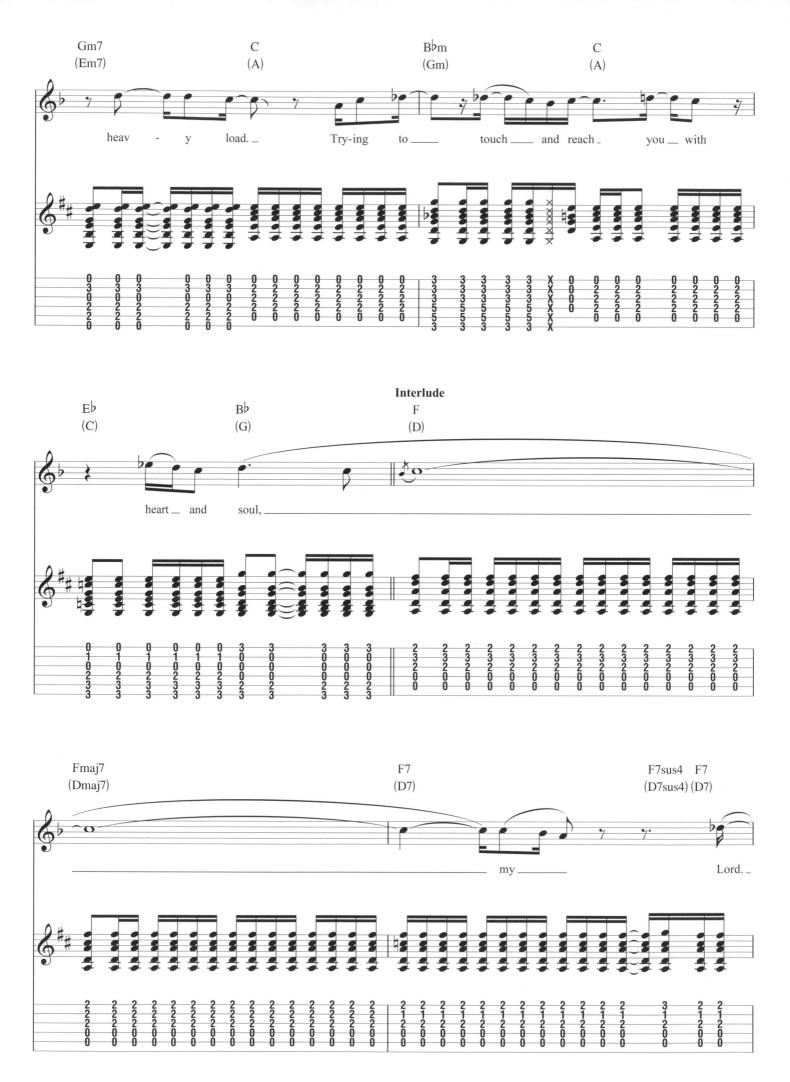

Gm7 C B♭m C
(Em7) (A) (Gm) (A)

heav - y load. __ Try-ing to ____ touch ____ and reach _ you _ with

E♭ B♭ **Interlude** F
(C) (G) (D)

heart _ and soul, _____

Fmaj7 F7 F7sus4 F7
(Dmaj7) (D7) (D7sus4) (D7)

_____ my _____ Lord. _

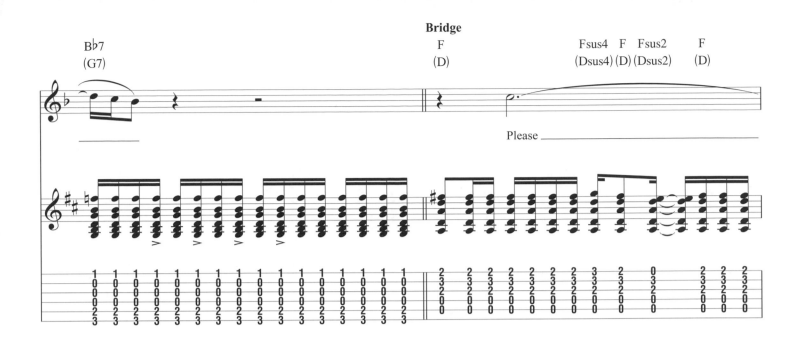

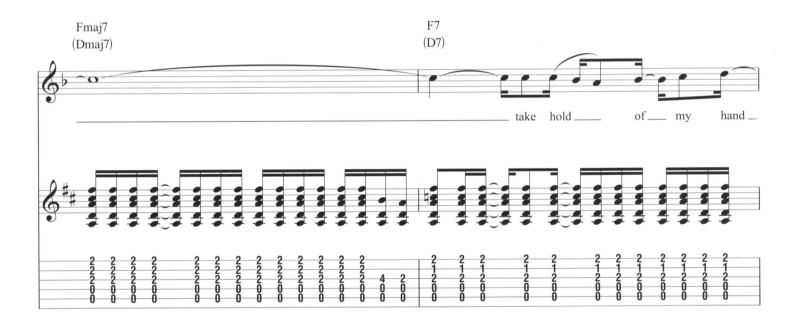

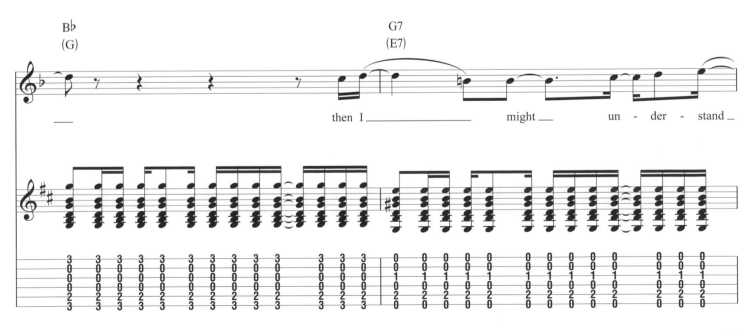

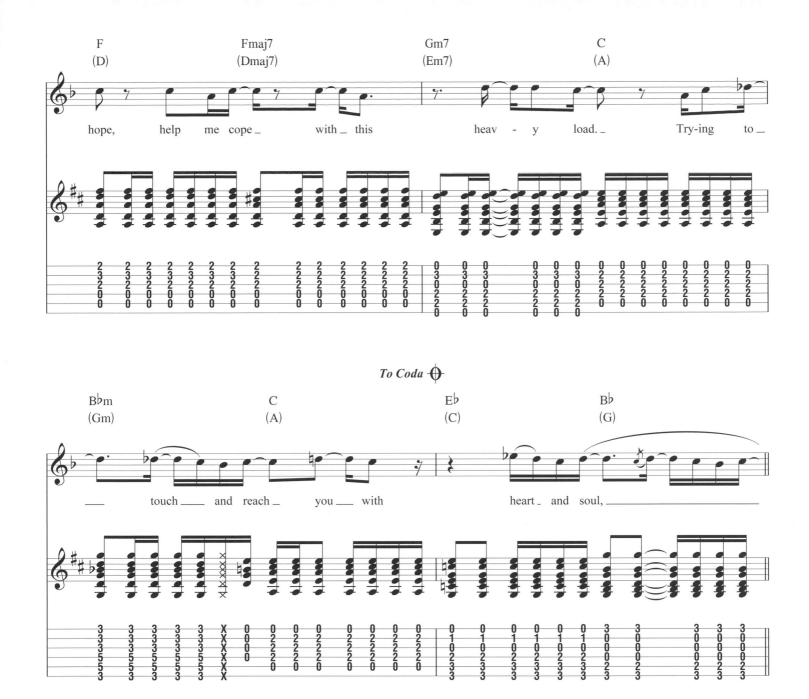

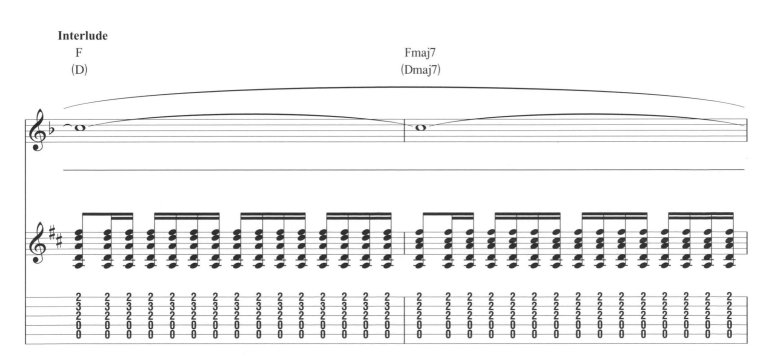

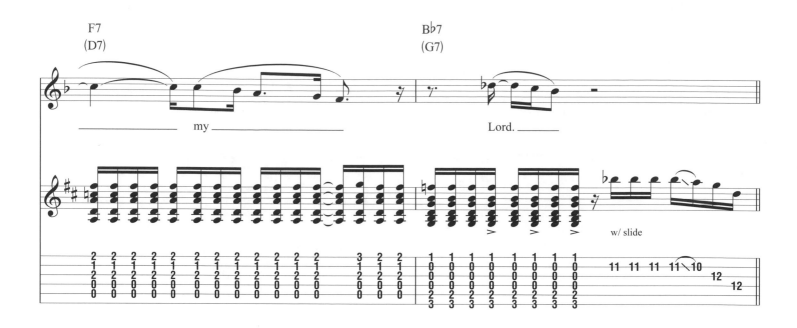

Guitar Solo

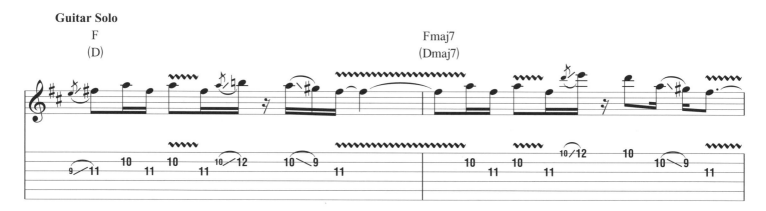

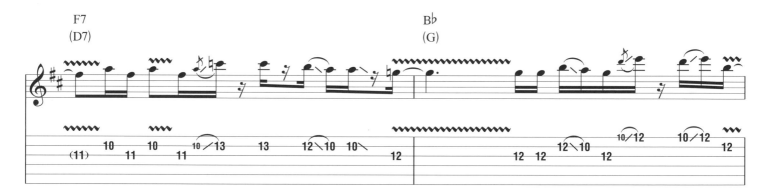

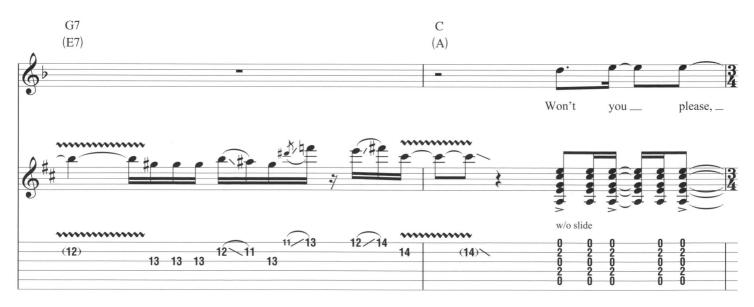

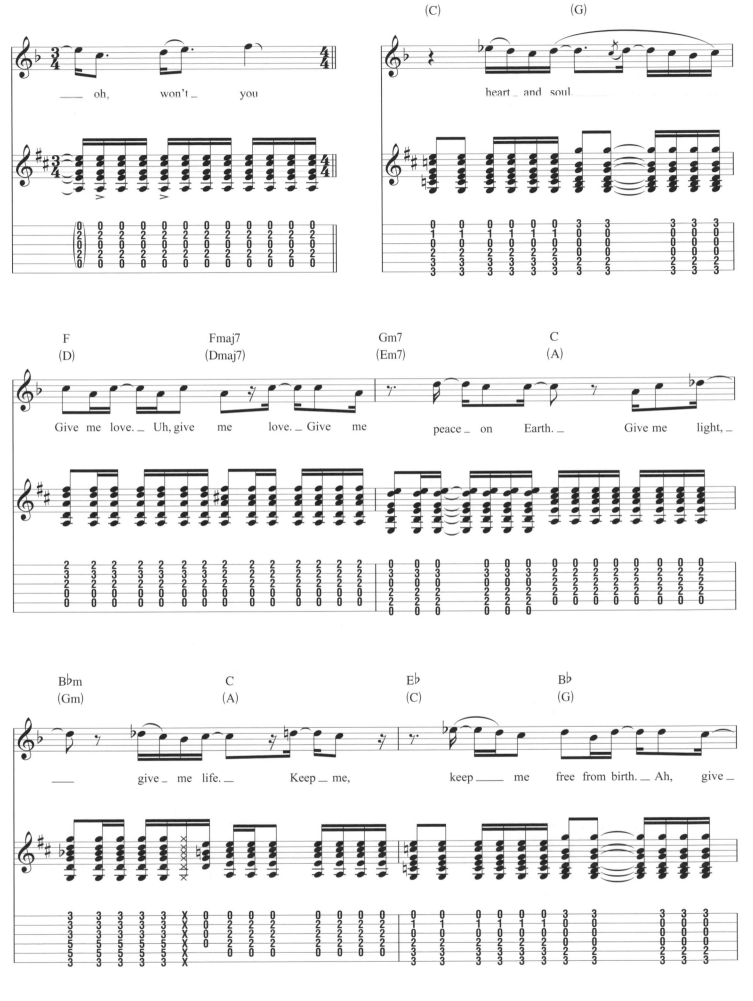

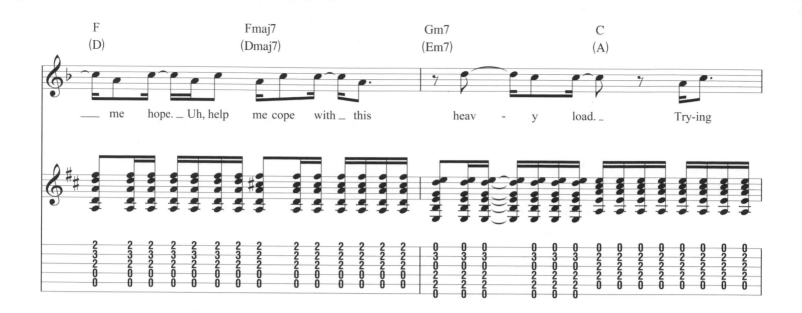

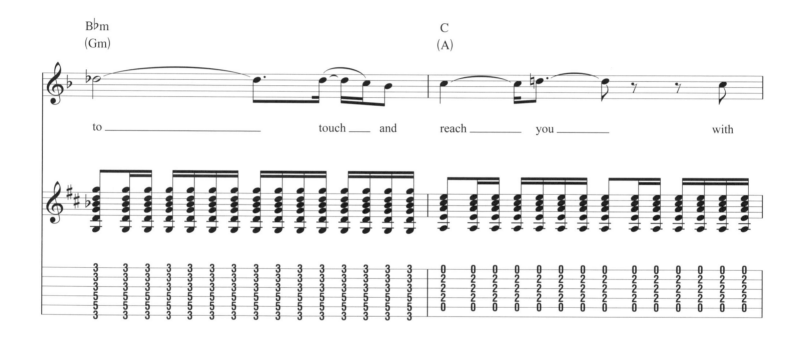

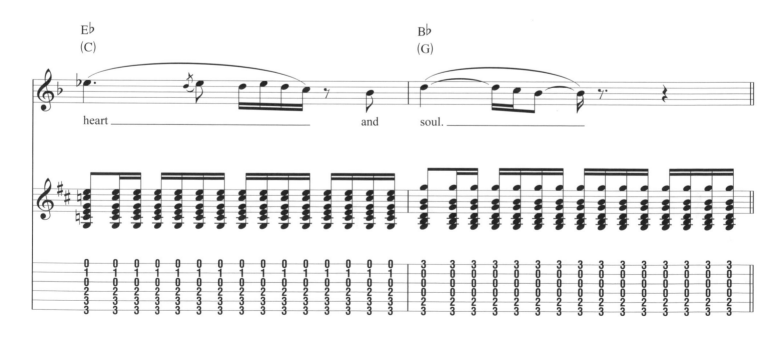

28

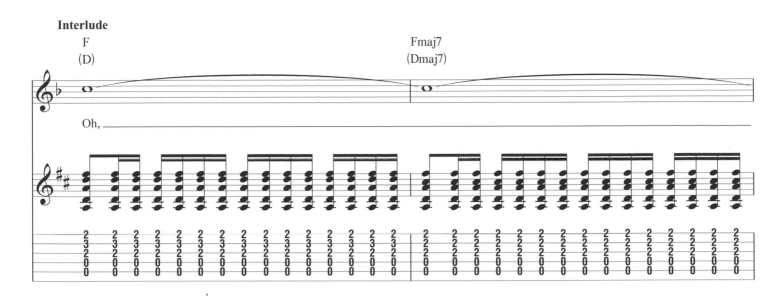

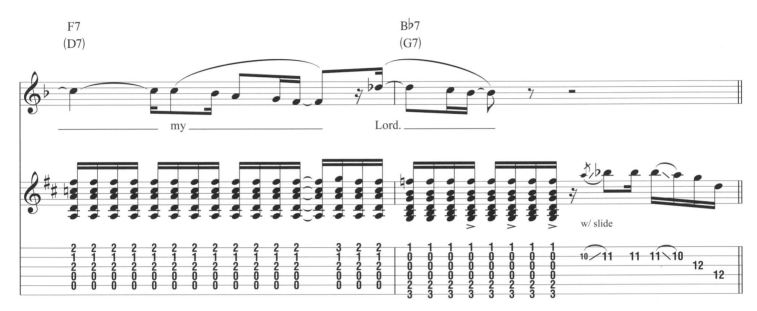

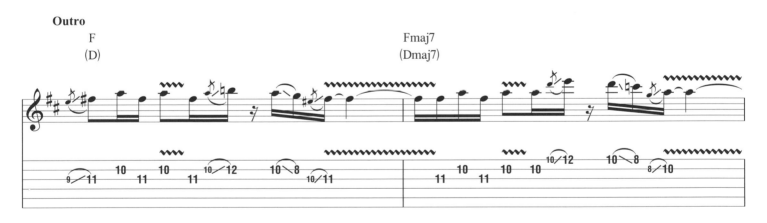

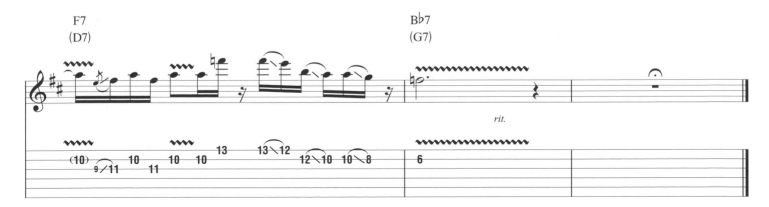

Here Comes the Sun

Words and Music by George Harrison

Capo VII

Intro

Moderately fast ♩ = 132

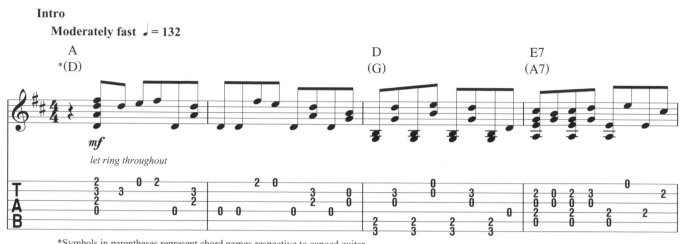

*Symbols in parentheses represent chord names respective to capoed guitar.
Symbols above reflect actual sounding chords. Capoed fret is "0" in tab.

Chorus

Here comes the sun, ____ doo, 'n' doo, doo, here comes the sun _

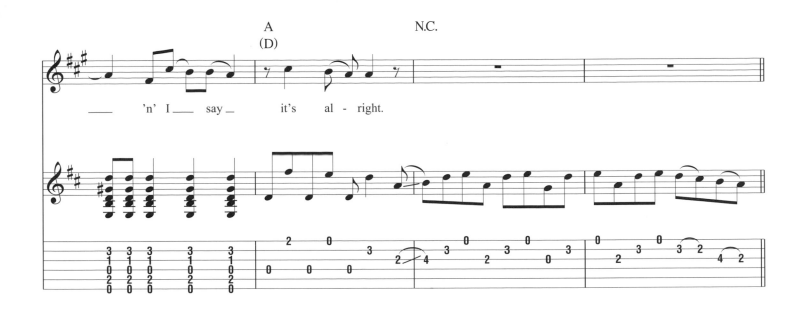

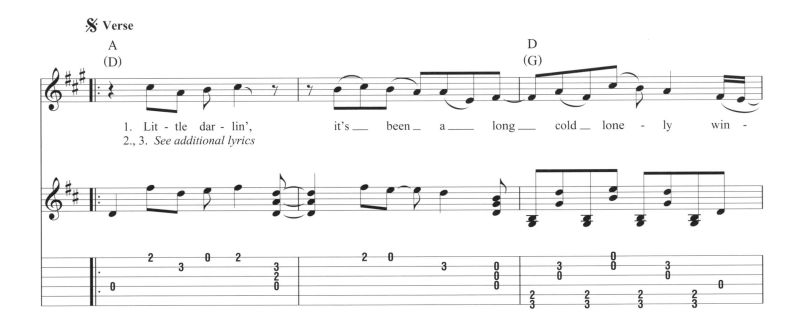

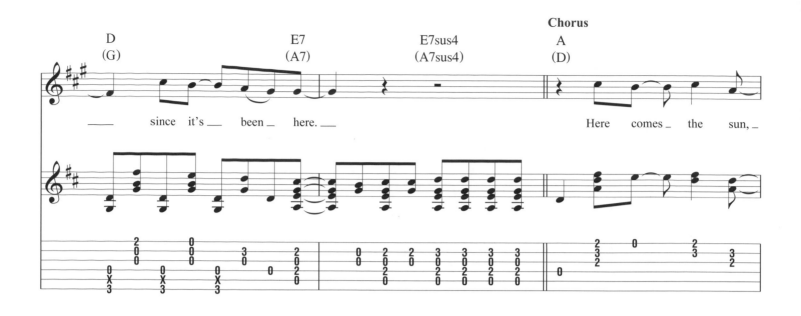

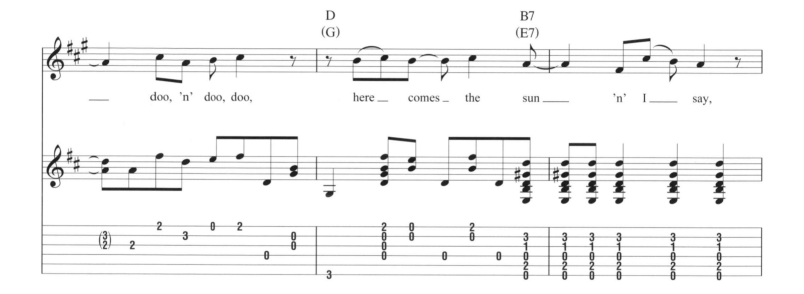

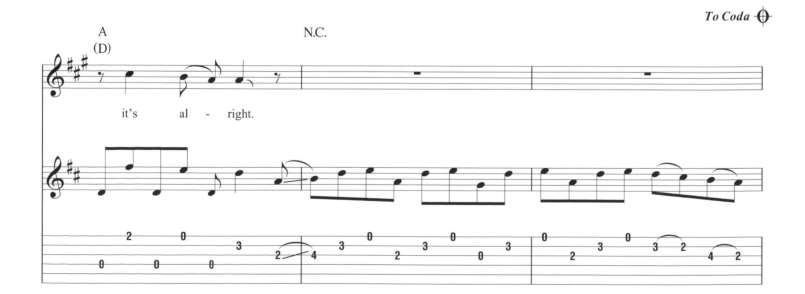

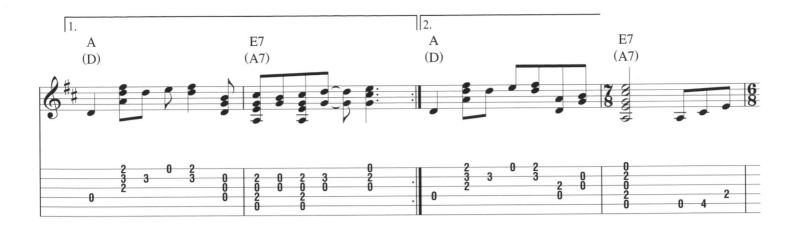

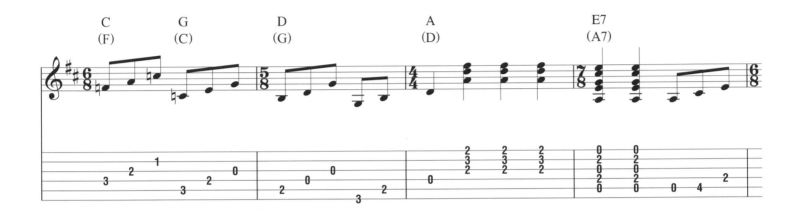

Sun, sun, sun, here it comes. __

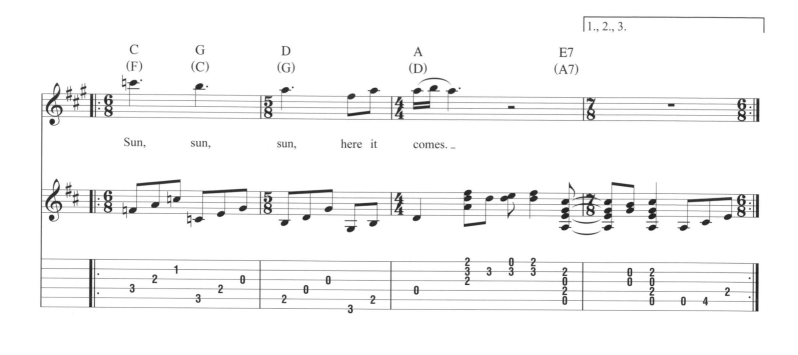

1., 2., 3.

C   G   D   A   E7
(F)   (C)   (G)   (D)   (A7)

Sun,   sun,   sun,   here it   comes. __

4.

D.S. al Coda

E7sus4   E7   E
(A7sus4)   (A7)   (A)

Coda

A   D   B7
(D)   (G)   (E7)

Here comes __ the   sun, __   doo, 'n' doo, doo,   here __ comes __ the   sun. __

Additional Lyrics

2. Little darling,
   The smiles returning to their faces;
   Little darling,
   It seems like years since it's been here.

3. Little darling,
   I feel that ice is slowly melting;
   Little darling,
   It seems like years since it's been clear.

Something

Words and Music by George Harrison

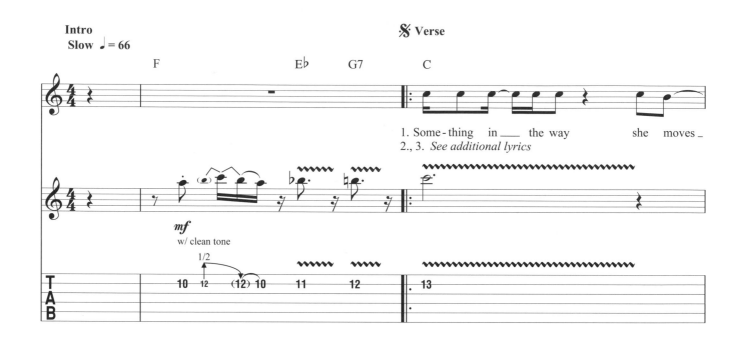

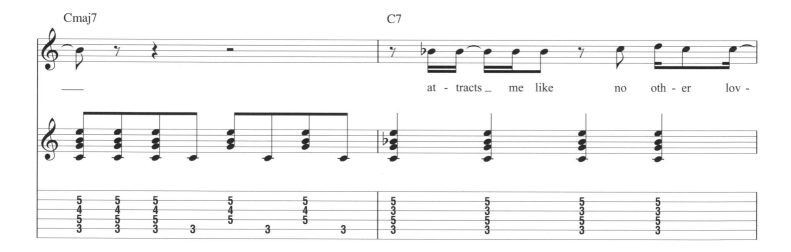

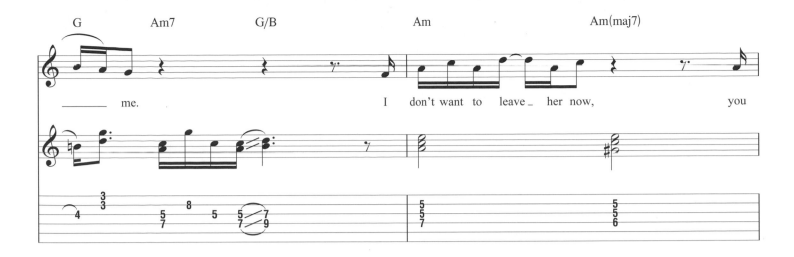

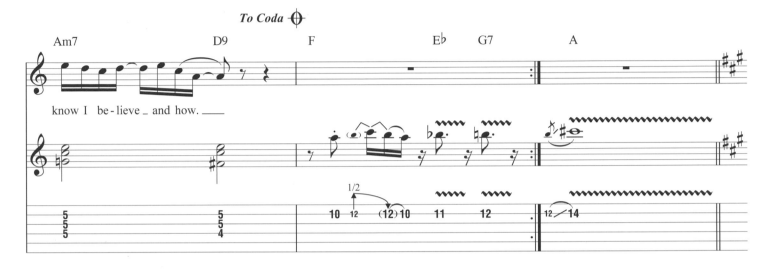

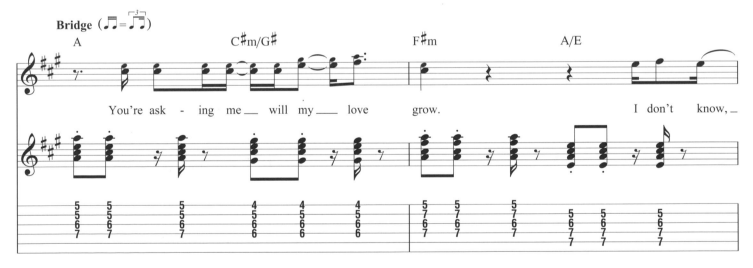

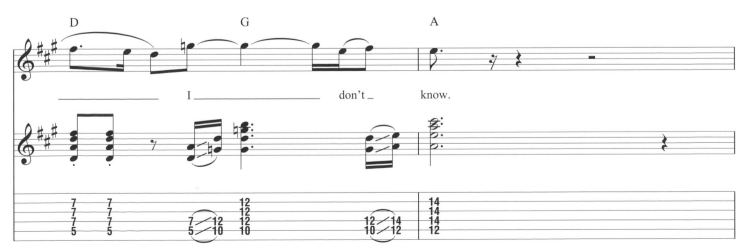

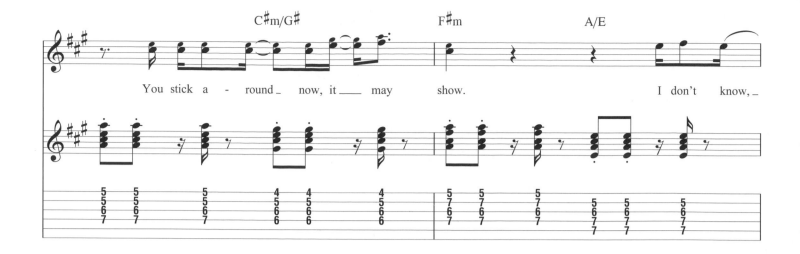

You stick a - round __ now, it __ may show. I don't know, __

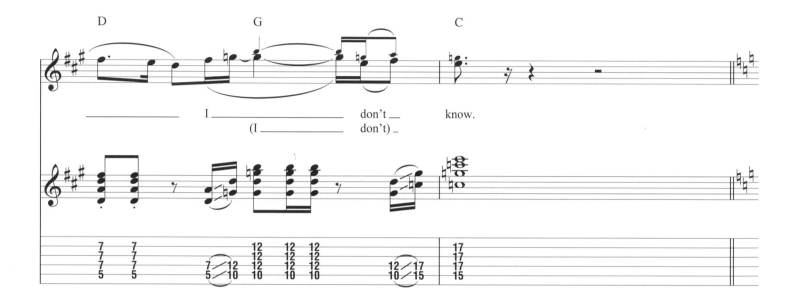

__ I __ don't __ know.
(I __ don't) _

Guitar Solo (♫ = ♫)

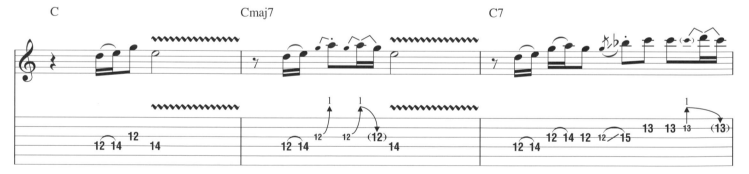

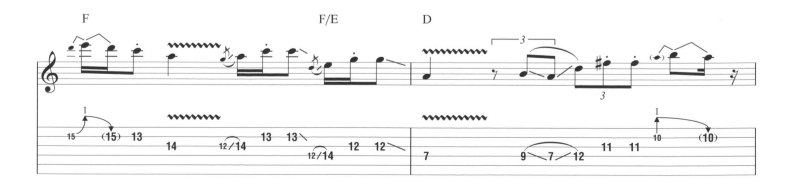

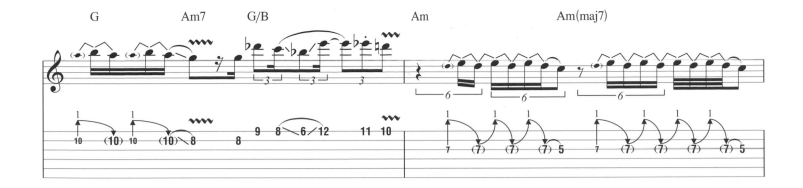

D.S. al Coda

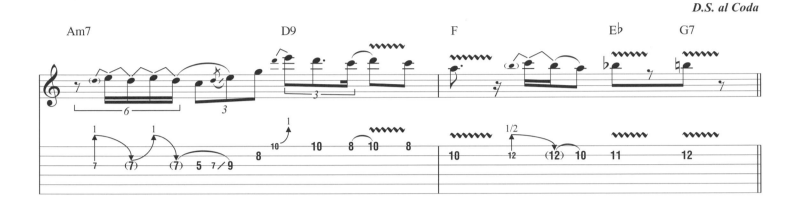

⊕ Coda

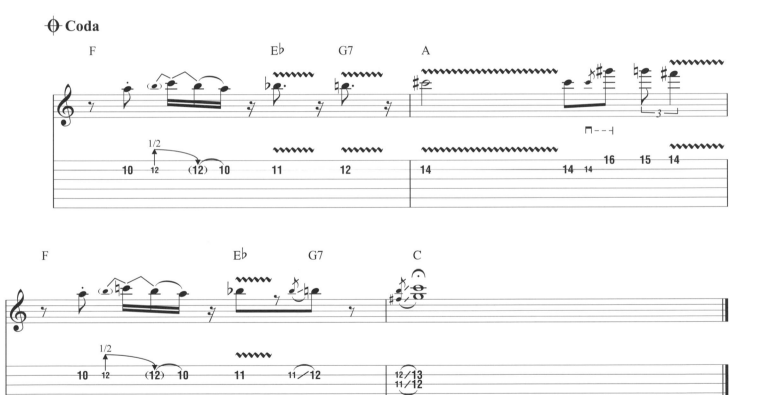

Additional Lyrics

2. Somewhere in her smile she knows
That I don't need no other lover.
Something in her style that shows me.
I don't want to leave her now,
You know I believe and how.

3. Something in the way she knows,
And all I have to do is think of her.
Something in the things she shows me.
I don't want to leave her now,
You know I believe and how.

What Is Life

Words and Music by George Harrison

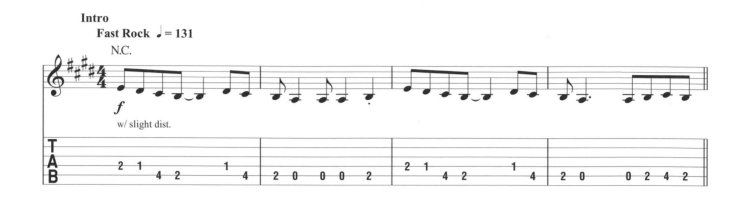

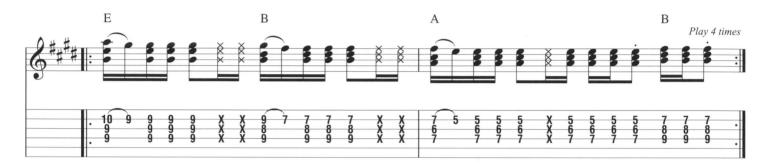

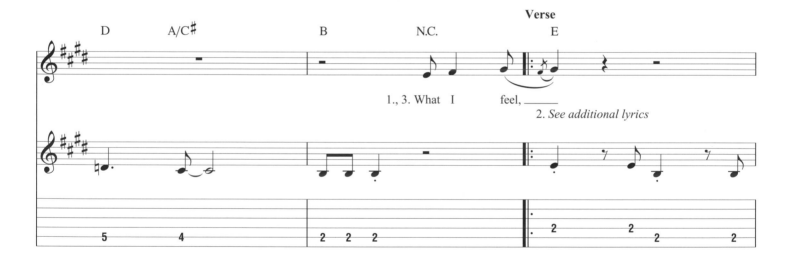

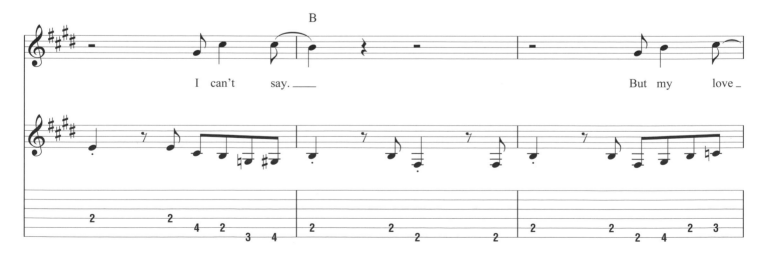

is there for you an-y time of day.

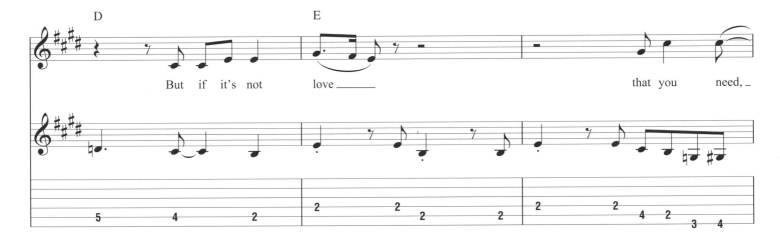

But if it's not love that you need,

then I'll try my best to make

ev-'ry-thing suc - ceed. Tell me,

Chorus

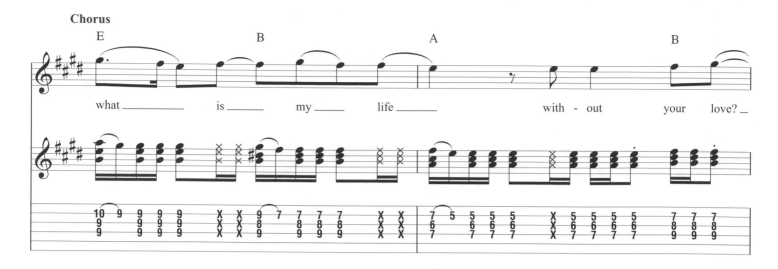

what _____ is _____ my _____ life _____ with - out your love? _

_____ And tell me,

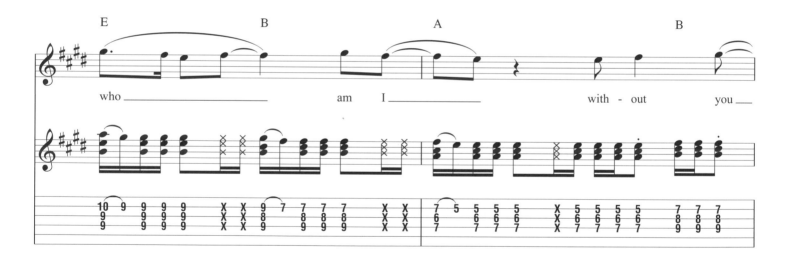

who _____ am I _____ with - out you _

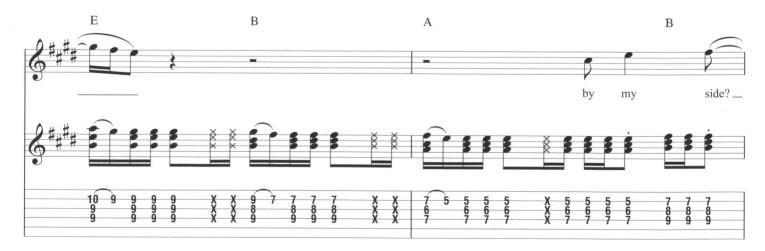

_____ by my side? _

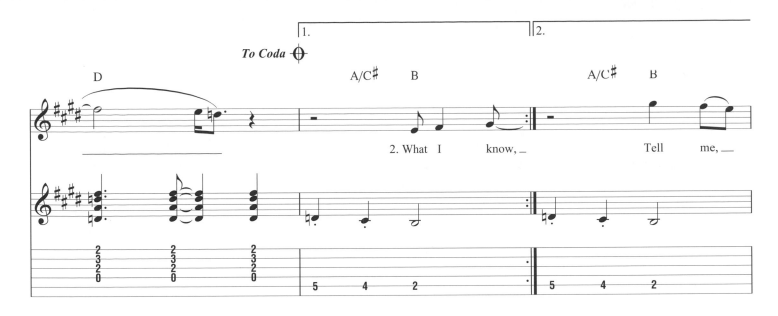

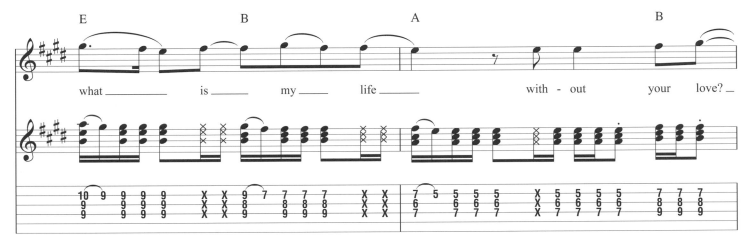

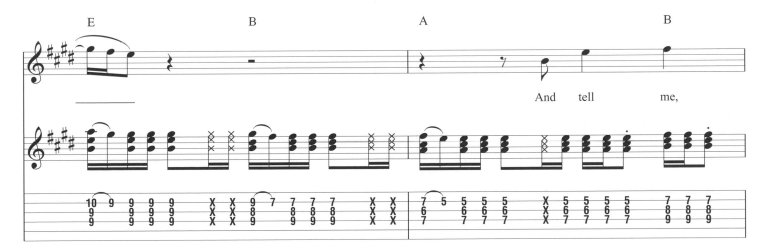

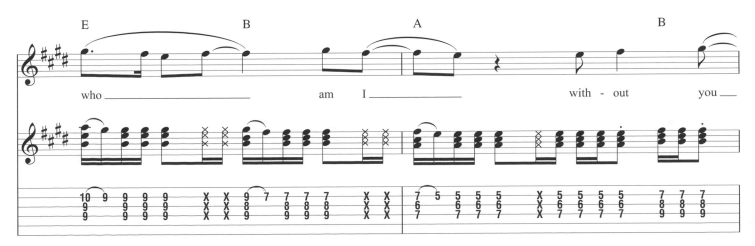

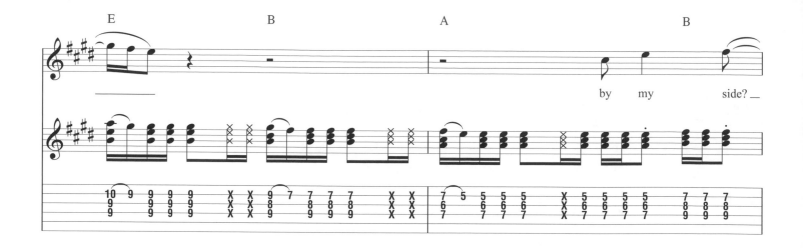

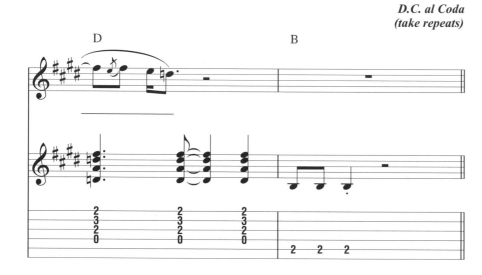

D.C. al Coda
(take repeats)

⊕ Coda

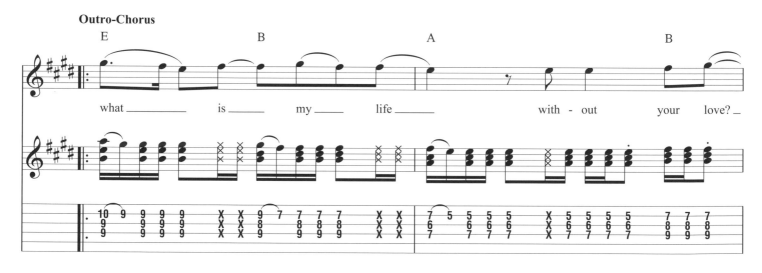

Outro-Chorus

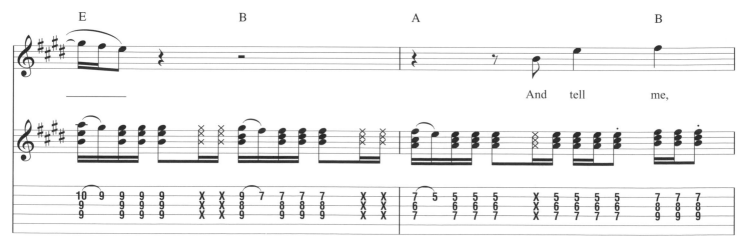

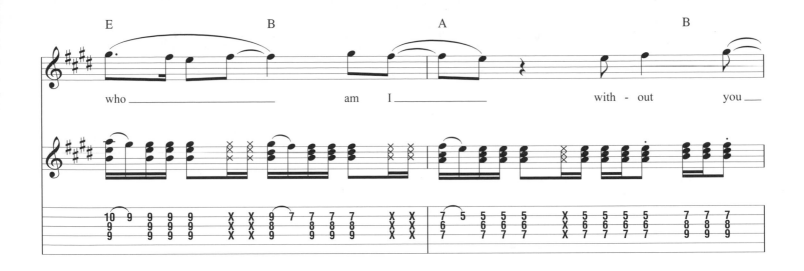

who _____ am I _____ with - out you ____

____ by my side? __

Repeat and fade

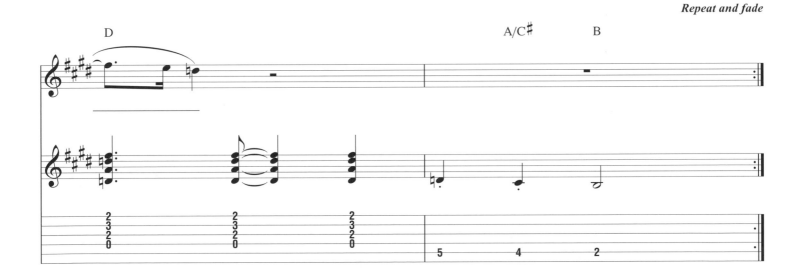

Additional Lyrics

2. What I know, I can do.
   If I give my love out to ev'ryone like you.
   But if it's not love that you need,
   Then I'll try my best to make ev'rything succeed.

While My Guitar Gently Weeps

Words and Music by George Harrison

Intro
Moderately ♩ = 114
Half-time feel

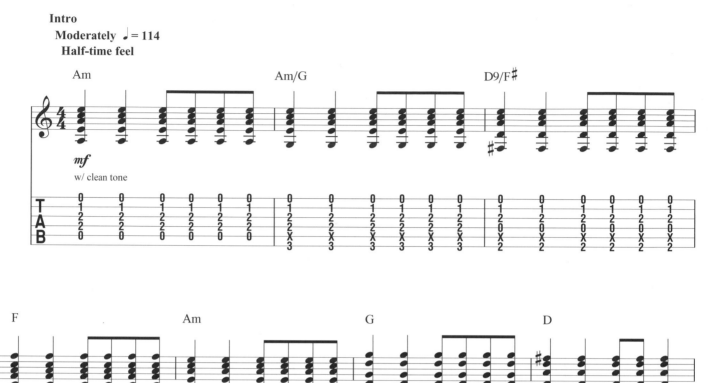

Verse

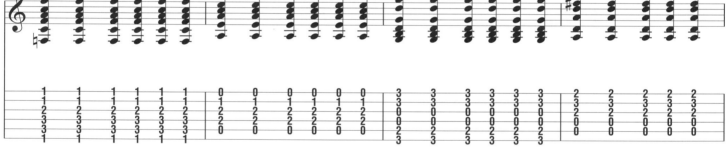

1. I look _____ at _____ you all, _____ see the love _____

w/ slight dist.

w/ clean tone

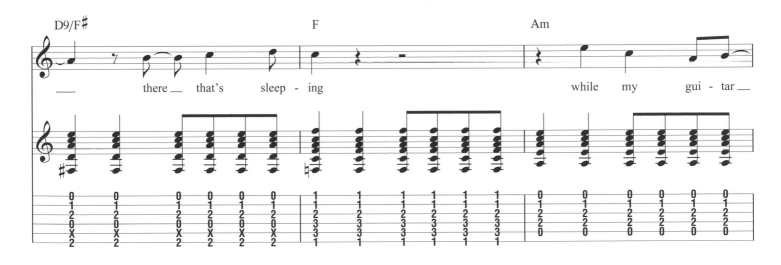

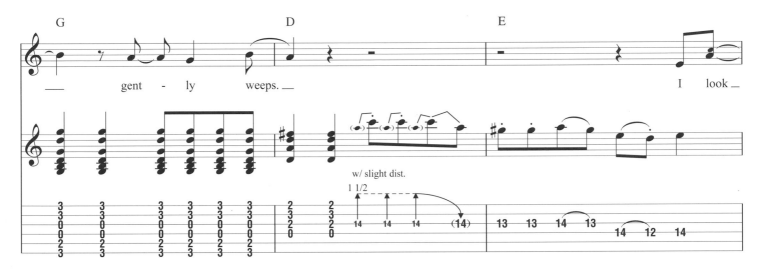

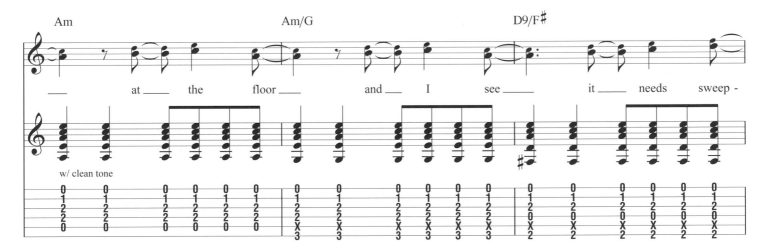

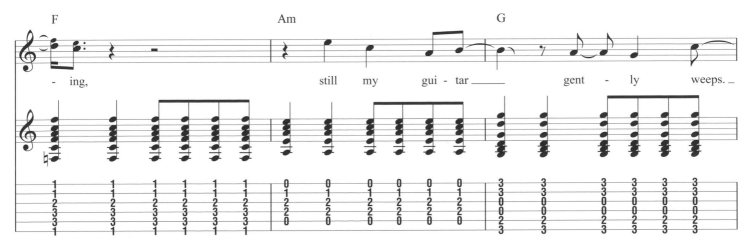

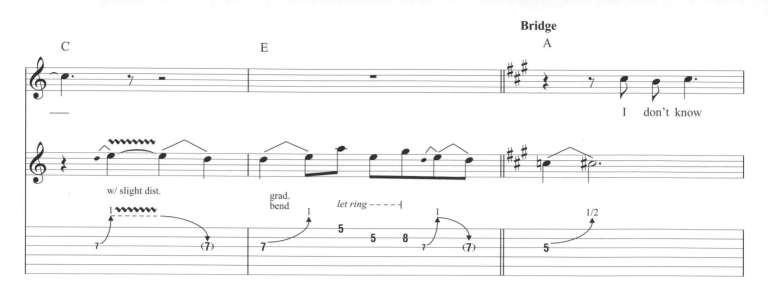

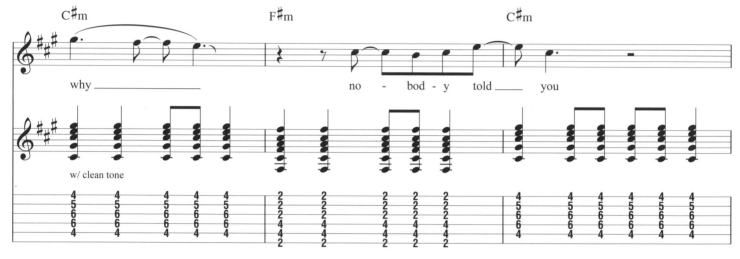

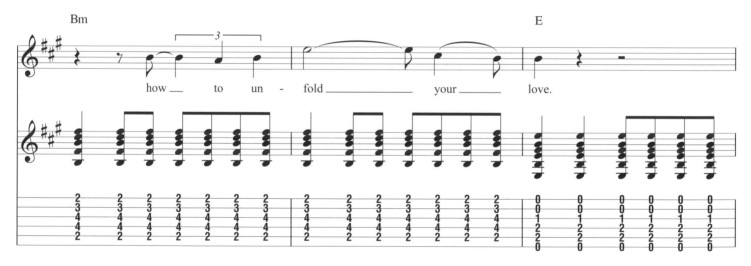

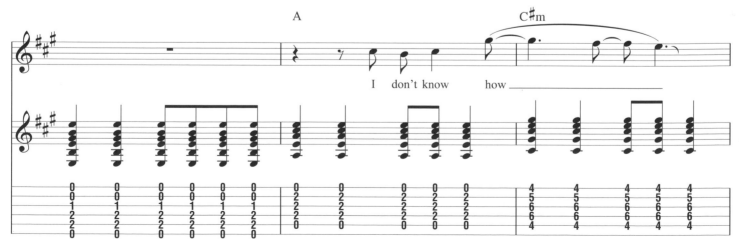

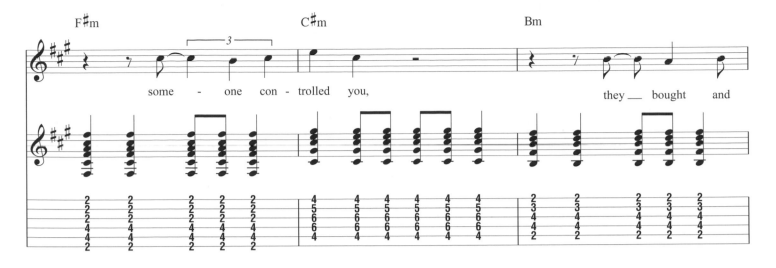

some - one con - trolled you, they __ bought and

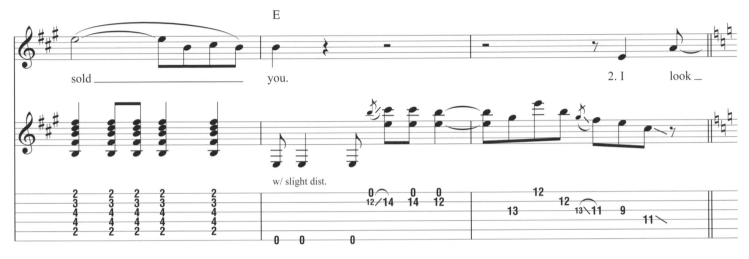

sold _____ you. 2. I look __

Verse

__ at __ the world __ and I no - tice __ it's turn -

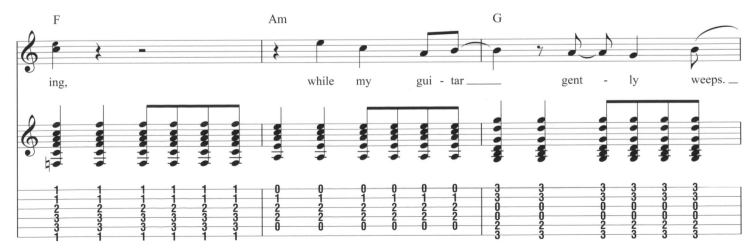

ing, while my gui - tar _____ gent - ly weeps. __

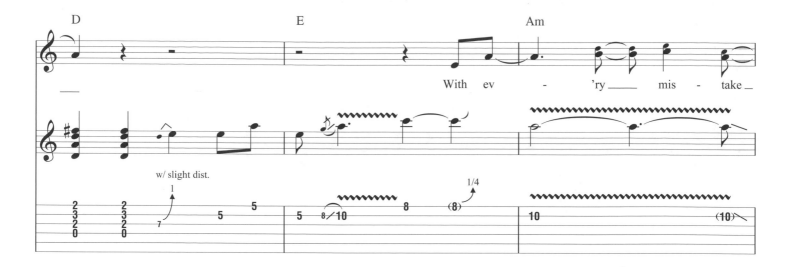

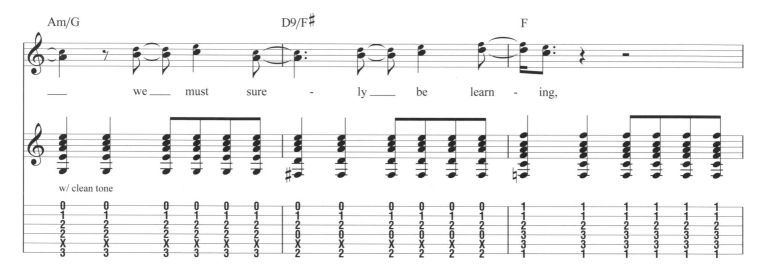

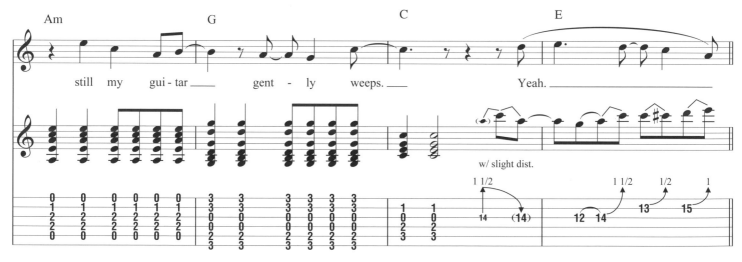

Guitar Solo

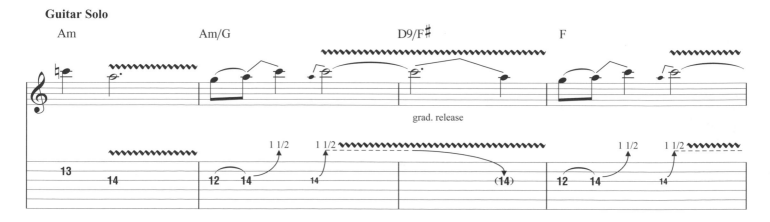

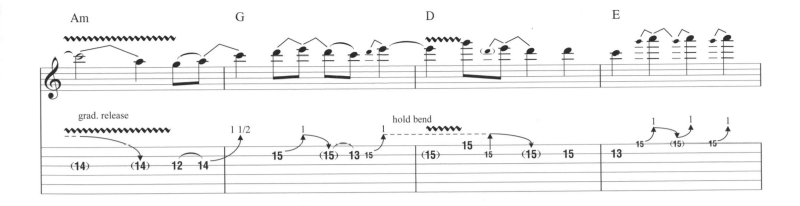

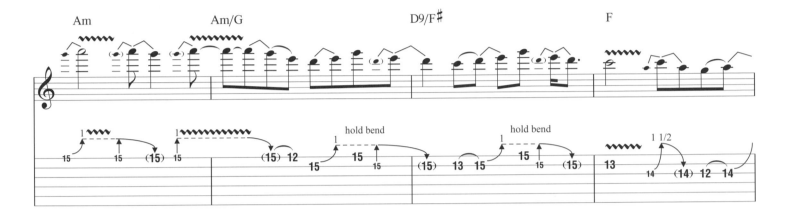

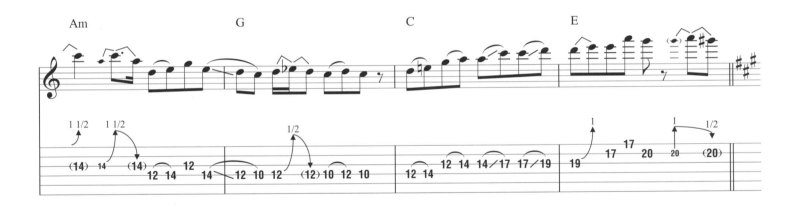

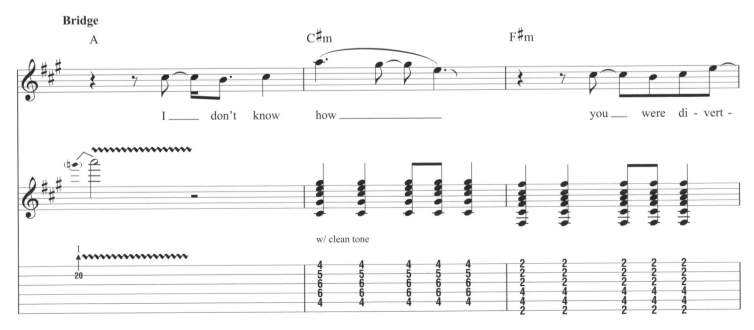

I ___ don't know how _____ you ___ were di - vert -

w/ clean tone

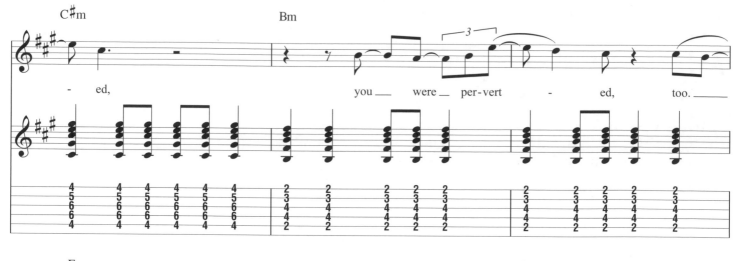

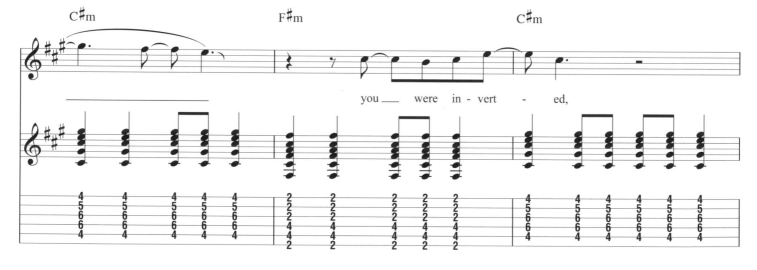

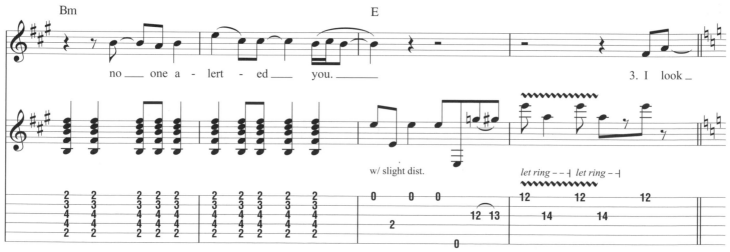

Verse

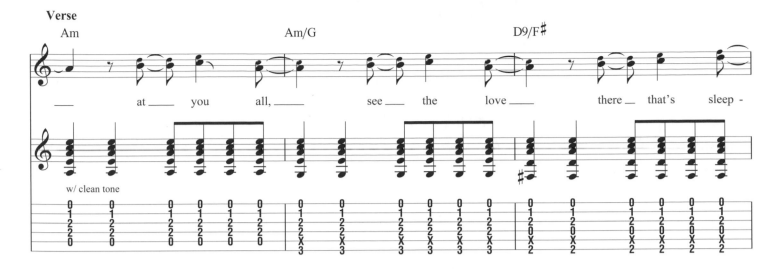

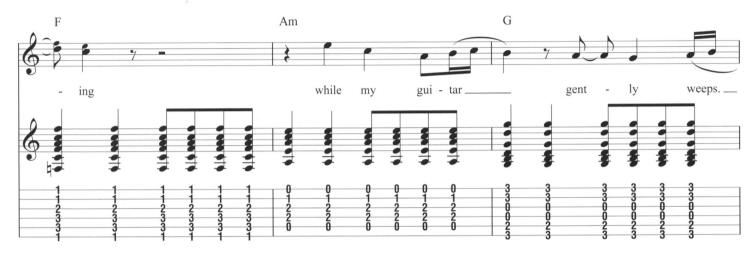

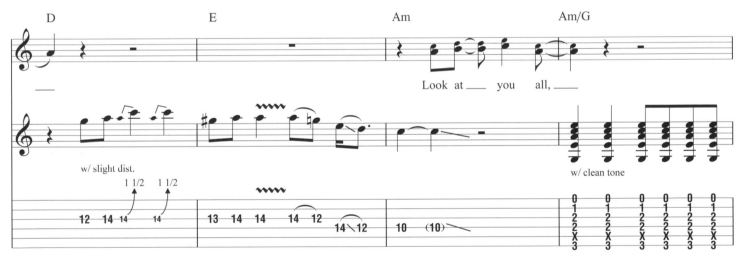

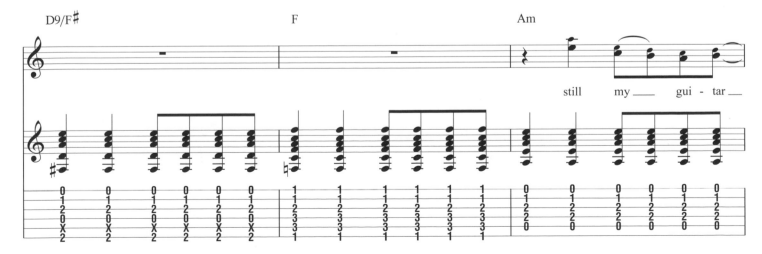

Outro-Guitar Solo

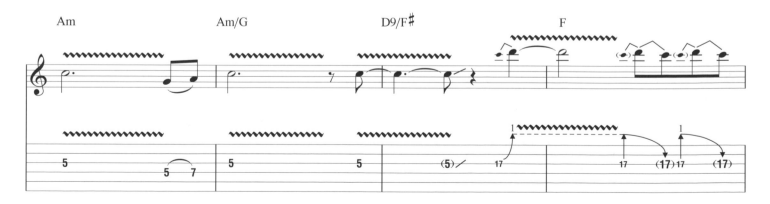

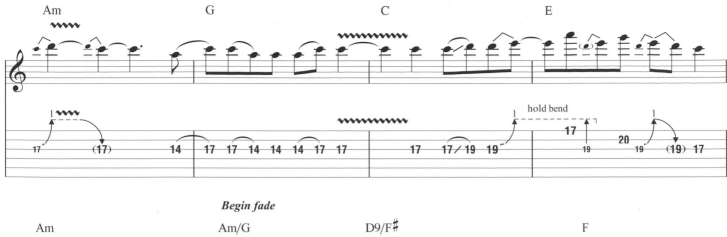

Begin fade

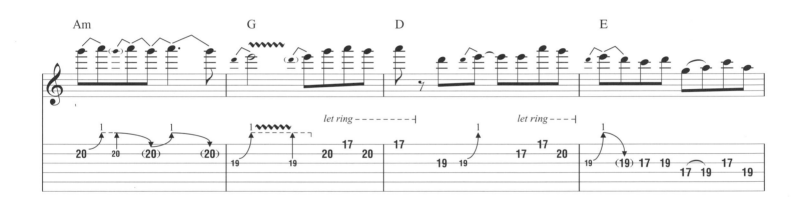

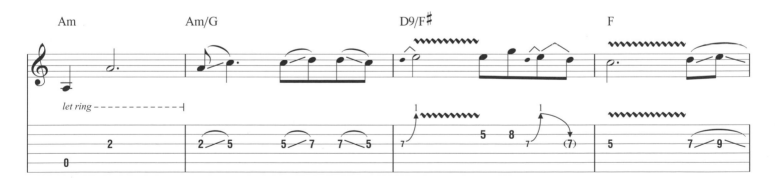

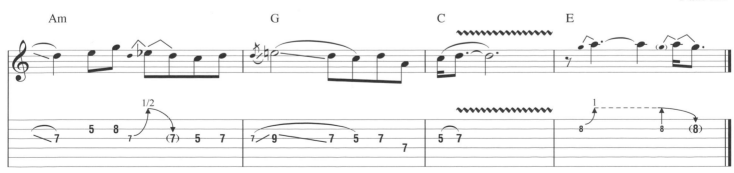

Fade out

GUITAR NOTATION LEGEND

THE MUSICAL STAFF shows pitches and rhythms and is divided by bar lines into measures. Pitches are named after the first seven letters of the alphabet.

TABLATURE graphically represents the guitar fingerboard. Each horizontal line represents a string, and each number represents a fret.

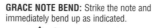

4th string, 2nd fret | 1st & 2nd strings open, played together | open D chord

HALF-STEP BEND: Strike the note and bend up 1/2 step.

WHOLE-STEP BEND: Strike the note and bend up one step.

GRACE NOTE BEND: Strike the note and immediately bend up as indicated.

SLIGHT (MICROTONE) BEND: Strike the note and bend up 1/4 step.

BEND AND RELEASE: Strike the note and bend up as indicated, then release back to the original note. Only the first note is struck.

PRE-BEND: Bend the note as indicated, then strike it.

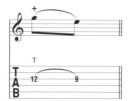

VIBRATO: The string is vibrated by rapidly bending and releasing the note with the fretting hand.

PALM MUTING: The note is partially muted by the pick hand lightly touching the string(s) just before the bridge.

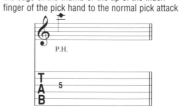

HAMMER-ON: Strike the first (lower) note with one finger, then sound the higher note (on the same string) with another finger by fretting it without picking.

PULL-OFF: Place both fingers on the notes to be sounded. Strike the first note and without picking, pull the finger off to sound the second (lower) note.

LEGATO SLIDE: Strike the first note and then slide the same fret-hand finger up or down to the second note. The second note is not struck.

SHIFT SLIDE: Same as legato slide, except the second note is struck.

TRILL: Very rapidly alternate between the notes indicated by continuously hammering on and pulling off.

TAPPING: Hammer ("tap") the fret indicated with the pick-hand index or middle finger and pull off to the note fretted by the fret hand.

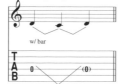

NATURAL HARMONIC: Strike the note while the fret-hand lightly touches the string directly over the fret indicated.

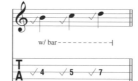

PINCH HARMONIC: The note is fretted normally and a harmonic is produced by adding the edge of the thumb or the tip of the index finger of the pick hand to the normal pick attack.

TREMOLO PICKING: The note is picked as rapidly and continuously as possible.

VIBRATO BAR DIVE AND RETURN: The pitch of the note or chord is dropped a specified number of steps (in rhythm), then returned to the original pitch.

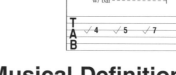

VIBRATO BAR SCOOP: Depress the bar just before striking the note, then quickly release the bar.

VIBRATO BAR DIP: Strike the note and then immediately drop a specified number of steps, then release back to the original pitch.

Additional Musical Definitions

 *(accent)*	• Accentuate note (play it louder).	

(staccato) • Play the note short.

D.S. al Coda • Go back to the sign (%), then play until the measure marked "*To Coda*," then skip to the section labelled "**Coda**."

D.C. al Fine • Go back to the beginning of the song and play until the measure marked "*Fine*" (end).

Fill • Label used to identify a brief melodic figure which is to be inserted into the arrangement.

N.C. • Harmony is implied.

 • Repeat measures between signs.

 • When a repeated section has different endings, play the first ending only the first time and the second ending only the second time.